Papatango Theatre Company

The world premiere

HANNA

by Sam Potter

First performance at Arcola Theatre, London:
Wednesday 3 January 2018

HANNA

by Sam Potter

Cast

Hanna	**Sophie Khan Levy**

Director	**George Turvey**
Designer	**Jasmine Swan**
Lighting Designer	**Jack Weir**
Music and Sound Designer	**Richard Hammarton**
Producer	**Chris Foxon**
Production Manager	**Ian Taylor for eStage Production**
Stage Manager	**Roisin Symes**
Tour Stage Manager	**Phil Glenny**

The performance lasts approximately 70 minutes.

There will be no interval.

BIOGRAPHIES

Sophie Khan Levy | Hanna
Sophie trained at the Guildhall School of Music and Drama.

Theatre credits include *Fracked* (Chichester Festival Theatre/national tour); *A Midsummer Night's Dream*, *The Christmas Truce*, *Love's Labour's Lost* and *Love's Labour's Won* (RSC) and *Cymbeline* (Belgrade Theatre, Coventry).

Radio credits include *Pilgrim's Progress*.

Sam Potter | Playwright
Sam is a writer and director. She was Papatango's Resident Playwright for 2015, supported by the BBC Performing Arts Fund.

Sam trained at Dartington College of Arts, Trinity College Dublin, the National Theatre and the RSC. As a director, she has worked at Hampstead Theatre, Trafalgar Studios, RSC, National Theatre and Glyndebourne Opera.

Her debut play, *Mucky Kid*, opened at Theatre503 in 2013 and saw her shortlisted for the Off West End Award for Most Promising New Playwright and earn a place on the 2015 Channel 4 Playwrights' Scheme with Papatango.

Writing credits include *Tuesday Play* (Daily Plays by Etch, Squint, Pleasance Theatre), *Daniel* (New Plays Festival, Tricycle Theatre) and *The Same Old Same Old Same* (Oxford School of Drama, Soho Theatre).

In 2016 she was one of five writers invited to take part in the Tricycle Theatre's inaugural New Writers' Programme NW6, and in 2017 she was the Writer in Residence at the North Wall Arts Centre in Oxford.

George Turvey | Director
George co-founded Papatango in 2007 and became the sole Artistic Director in January 2013.

Credits as director include *The Annihilation of Jessie Leadbeater* (Papatango at ALRA); *After Independence* (Papatango at Arcola Theatre/BBC Radio Four; 2016 Alfred Fagon Audience Award); *Leopoldville* (Papatango at Tristan Bates Theatre) and *Angel* (Papatango at Pleasance London/Tristan Bates Theatre).

George trained as an actor at the Academy of Live and Recorded Arts (ALRA) and has appeared on stage and screen throughout the UK and internationally, including the lead roles in the world premiere of Arthur Miller's *No Villain* (Old Red Lion Theatre/Trafalgar Studios) and *Batman Live World Arena Tour*.

As a dramaturg, he has led the development of all of Papatango's productions. He is co-writing *Being a Playwright: A Career Guide for Writers*, due for publication in 2018.

Jasmine Swan | Designer

Jasmine trained at Liverpool Institute for Performing Arts, graduating in 2016 with a First Class BA Hons in Theatre Performance Design.

Theatre as designer includes *The Passing of the Third Floor Back* (Finborough Theatre); *Hyem* (Theatre503/Northern Stage); *Fundraising Quiz Night* (reopening of the Bush Theatre); *Scene Change Presents: Coming of Age* (Liverpool Playhouse Studio); *Who's Afraid of the Working Class?* (Unity Theatre); *The Wonderful World of Dissocia* (Liverpool Playhouse Studio); *Next Door But One* (Cornerstone Theatre, Liverpool) and *Animal Farm* (Tell Tale Theatre).

Site-specific work includes co-designing immersive performance art event *Subterrania* (Palm House, Liverpool) and *Fiesta Bombarda* (Constellations, Liverpool).

She has assisted fashion set designer Shona Heath and worked as a modelmaker to Andrew D Edwards, Frankie Bradshaw, Andrew Riley, David Woodhead, Christopher Oram and Paul Wills, and was recently a finalist in the Linbury Prize for Stage Design 2017, working with Phoenix Dance Theatre based in Leeds. She is currently the Laboratory Associate Designer for Nuffield Southampton Theatres 2017/18.

Jack Weir | Lighting Designer

Jack was nominated for the 2016 WhatsOnStage award for Best Lighting Design for *The Boys in the Band* at the Vaudeville Theatre, West End. He was also double-nominated and a finalist in the Off West End Awards for Best Lighting Designer in the same year.

He trained at the Guildhall School of Music and Drama and won the ETC award for lighting design in 2014.

Some of his recent work includes *George's Marvellous Medicine* (Leicester Curve Theatre/UK tour); *Pyar Actually* (Watford Palace/UK tour); *Talk Radio* (Old Red Lion Theatre); *Assata Taught Me* (Gate Theatre); *Holding the Man* (Above The Stag); *Salad Days* (Union Theatre); *Dust* (Underbelly); *Summer in London* (Theatre Royal Stratford East); *Judy!* (The Arts Theatre, West End); *Betty Blue Eyes* (Chichester University); *CAT! – The Play* (Ambassadors Theatre, West End); *The Plague* (Arcola Theatre); *Ray Cooney's Out of Order* (Yvonne Arnaud Theatre/UK tour); *Pray So Hard For You* and *Princess Caraboo* (Finborough Theatre); *La Ronde* (The Bunker); *The Boys in the Band* (Vaudeville Theatre, West End); *Through the Mill* (Southwark Playhouse); *No Villain* and *My Children! My Africa!* (Trafalgar Studios); *Little Voice, Bad Girls, Road Show* and *The Spitfire Grill* (Union Theatre); *Four Play* (Theatre503); *African Gothic* (Park Theatre) and *The Pirates of Penzance* (UK tour).

Richard Hammarton | Music and Sound Designer

Theatre includes *Trestle*, *Orca* and *Tomcat* (Papatango at Southwark Playhouse); *After Independence* (Papatango at Arcola Theatre); *Girls* (HighTide Festival Theatre and Soho Theatre); *Burning Doors* (Belarus Free Theatre); *Much Ado About Nothing* and *Jumpy* (Theatr Clwyd); *Linda* (Royal Court Theatre); *The Crucible*, *Brilliant Adventures*, *Edward II* and *Dr Faustus* (Royal Exchange Theatre, Manchester); *As You Like It* (Shared Experience); *A Number* (Nuffield Theatre/ Young Vic); *The Weir* (English Touring Theatre); *Comrade Fiasco* (Gate Theatre); *Grimm Tales 2* (Bargehouse, Oxo Tower Wharf); *The Pitchfork Disney* and *Ghost from a Perfect Place* (Arcola Theatre); *The Crucible* (Old Vic); *Dealer's Choice* (Royal & Derngate Theatre); *Kingston 14* (Theatre Royal Stratford East); *Deposit* and *Fault Lines* (Hampstead Theatre); *Early Days (of a Better Nation)* (Battersea Arts Centre); *Sizwe Bansi is Dead* and *Six Characters Looking for an Author* (Young Vic); *The Taming of the Shrew* (Shakespeare's Globe); *Speaking in Tongues* (Duke of York's Theatre); *A Raisin in the Sun* (Lyric Hammersmith/national tour); *Mudlarks* (HighTide Festival/Theatre503/Bush Theatre); *Ghosts* (Duchess Theatre); *Judgement Day* (The Print Room); *Persuasion*, *The Constant Wife*, *Les Liaisons Dangereuses*, *Arsenic and Old Lace*, *The Real Thing* and *People at Sea* (Salisbury Playhouse); *Platform* (Old Vic Tunnels); *Pride and Prejudice* (Theatre Royal Bath/ national tour); *Dealer's Choice* (Birmingham Rep); *Hello and Goodbye* and *Some Kind of Bliss* (Trafalgar Studios); *Breakfast with Mugabe* (Theatre Royal Bath) and Olivier Award-winner *The Mountaintop*, *In Event of Moone Disaster*, *Inches Apart*, *Ship of Fools*, *Natural Selection* and *Salt Meets Wound* (Theatre503).

Television includes *Ripper Street*, *Agatha Christie's Marple*, *No Win No Fee*, *Sex 'N' Death*, *Wipeout* and *The Ship*.

Orchestration includes *Agatha Christie's Marple*, *Primeval*, *Dracula*, *Jericho*, *If I Had You*, *A History of Britain*, *Silent Witness*, *Dalziel and Pascoe*, *Alice Through the Looking Glass*, *The Nine Lives of Tomas Katz* and *Scenes of a Sexual Nature*.

Chris Foxon | Producer

Chris joined Papatango in 2012 and his productions with the company include *Trestle* (Papatango New Writing Prize 2017, Southwark Playhouse); *Orca* (Papatango New Writing Prize 2016, Southwark Playhouse); *After Independence* (Arcola Theatre, 2016 Alfred Fagon Audience Award); *Tomcat* (Papatango New Writing Prize 2015, Southwark Playhouse); *Coolatully* (Papatango New Writing Prize 2014, Finborough Theatre); *Unscorched* (Papatango New Writing Prize 2013, Finborough Theatre) and *Pack* and *Everyday Maps for Everyday Use* (Papatango New Writing Prize 2012, Finborough Theatre).

His other productions include *The Transatlantic Commissions* (Old Vic); *Donkey Heart* (Old Red Lion Theatre/Trafalgar Studios); *The Fear of Breathing* (Finborough Theatre; transferred in a new production to the Akasaka Red Theatre, Tokyo); *The Keepers of Infinite Space* (Park Theatre); *Happy New* (Trafalgar Studios); *Tejas Verdes* (Edinburgh Festival) and *The Madness of George III* (Oxford Playhouse).

Chris is a visiting lecturer at the Royal Central School of Speech and Drama and the University of York. He is co-writing *Being a Playwright: A Career Guide for Writers*, due for publication in 2018.

Production Acknowledgements

Image Design | **Rebecca Pitt**
Production Photography | **Robert Workman**
Press Representation | **Kate Morley PR**

Many thanks to our generous supporters: Arts Council England, Austin and Hope Pilkington Trust, Backstage Trust, Boris Karloff Charitable Foundation, Garfield Weston Foundation, Golsoncott Foundation, Harold Hyam Wingate Foundation, Mildred Duveen Charitable Trust, Leche Trust, and Kathryn Thompson.

We would like to thank our post-show partners, People in Harmony.

People in Harmony, an organisation for mixed race people, families and couples, has provided information and support for over 45 years. We aim to influence and improve ways in which public services such as education, health, social care and justice are delivered, using discussion, debate, research, campaigns and the arts.

'Remarkable unearthers of new talent' *Evening Standard*

Papatango discover and champion new playwrights through free, open application schemes and opportunities.

Our flagship programme is the Papatango New Writing Prize, the UK's only annual award guaranteeing an emerging playwright a full production, publication, 10% of the gross box office, and an unprecedented £6000 commission for a second play. The Prize is free to enter and assessed anonymously, and all entrants receive personal feedback on their scripts, an unmatched commitment to supporting aspiring playwrights. Over 1000 entries are received each year.

Writers discovered through the Prize have received Off West End and RNT Foundation Playwright Awards and BAFTAs, made work with the RSC, BBC, Hampstead Theatre, National Theatre, Out of Joint and other leading organisations, and premiered in over twenty countries.

Papatango also run an annual Resident Playwright scheme, taking an emerging playwright through commissioning, development and production of a new play. Our first Resident, May Sumbwanyambe, won the 2016 Alfred Fagon Audience Award for our production of *After Independence*, which we then adapted and produced for BBC Radio Four. Our second Resident, Sam Potter, won a place on the Channel 4 Playwright's Scheme with our backing.

Papatango launched a new arm in summer 2017 called GoWrite. GoWrite delivers an extensive programme of free playwriting opportunities for children and adults nationwide. Children in state schools write their own plays which are then professionally performed and published, while adults take part in workshops, complete six-month courses at a variety of regional venues culminating in free public performances, or join fortnightly one-to-one career facilitation services. GoWrite has delivered face-to-face training for over 2000 budding writers over the last year, with £5000 available in bursaries to enable in-need writers nationwide to access our opportunities.

10% of seats at our productions are donated to charities for young people at risk of exclusion from the arts.

All our opportunities are free and entered anonymously, encouraging the best new talent regardless of means or connections.

Papatango's motto is simple. All you need is a story.

Papatango are a registered charity.

We rely on the generous support of individuals as well as trusts and foundations. Any help in delivering our unprecedented programme of world premieres from brilliant artists who would otherwise go unseen makes a huge difference. You can help us to inspire grassroots writers that they too can break into theatre.

If you would like to support Papatango or perhaps get involved in a particular project, then please email **chris@papatango.co.uk**.

We make a little go a long way.

£5 buys a ticket for an in-need young person

£10 covers the cost of printing scripts for an entire cast

£20 funds the resources for a free writing workshop

£50 provides 25 free playtexts for school libraries

£75 pays for a day of rehearsals

£100 provides a full costume for a character on stage

£200 enables us to travel to run workshops across the UK

£500 pays for a special performance for a school group

£1000 funds a week of script R&D with actors and writer

£2000 supports a budding writer with a seed commission

£6000 commissions a full script from a new writer

£10,000 pays for a brilliant cast for a month long show

Every donation makes an enormous difference.

Online
For up-to-date news and opportunities please visit:
www.facebook.com/pages/PapaTango-Theatre-Company/257825071298
www.twitter.com/PapaTangoTC
www.papatango.co.uk

Papatango Theatre Company Ltd is a registered charity and a company limited by guarantee. Registered in England and Wales no. 07365398. Registered Charity no. 1152789.

arcola theatre

One of London's leading Off West End theatres

Bloomberg

Hackney

ARTS COUNCIL
ENGLAND

HANNA TOUR DATES

Arcola Theatre, London
3–20 January 2018
Press night: 5 January at 8 p.m.
www.arcolatheatre.com
Box Office: 020 7503 1646

Everyman Theatre, Cheltenham
22 & 23 January 2018
www.everymantheatre.org.uk
Box Office: 01242 572573

North Wall Arts Centre, Oxford
24 January 2018
www.thenorthwall.com
Box Office: 01865 319450

Marlowe Studio, Canterbury
25 January 2018
www.marlowetheatre.com
Box Office: 01227 787787

Quarry Theatre, Bedford
26 January 2018
www.quarrytheatre.org.uk
Box Office: 01234 362337

The Hat Factory, Luton
27 January 2018
www.lutonculture.com/hat-factory
Box Office: 01582 878100

The Bike Shed, Exeter
30 January–3 February 2018
www.bikeshedtheatre.co.uk
Box Office: 01392 434169

Theatr Clwyd, Mold
7 & 8 February 2018
www.theatrclwyd.com
Box Office: 01352 701521

The Hope Street Theatre, Liverpool
9 & 10 February 2018
www.hopestreettheatre.com
Box Office: 03333 443230

Greenwich Theatre, London
19–21 February 2018
www.greenwichtheatre.org.uk
Box Office: 020 8858 7755

Royal Welsh College of Music and Drama, Cardiff
22 February 2018
www.rwcmd.ac.uk/whatson
Box Office: 029 2039 1391

HANNA

Sam Potter

Acknowledgements

I would like to offer my heartfelt thanks to the following people:

To my wonderful agent, Kara. To Lisa (gone but not forgotten) and everyone at Alan Brodie. To George and Chris from Papatango. To Nadia Clifford for her generosity and wisdom during the first reading of the play. To Sophie for bringing Hanna to life. To Matt, Sarah Liisa and all at Nick Hern Books. To the Channel 4 Playwrights' Scheme and Joy and Alan Potter for supporting the writing of this play and lastly, my greatest thanks as always, go to Will, for everything.

S.P.

For Tom and George

Notes on the Text

The play should be presented as simply as possible on a bare stage. Hanna should speak directly to the audience.

Two question marks at the end of a sentence (??) indicate a rising inflection.

The name David is pronounced Daveede.

This text went to press before the end of rehearsals and so may differ slightly from the play as performed.

PART ONE

HANNA, *aged twenty-one*

When I tell people what happened, they always seem to think that it would have made such a big difference if we'd known sooner... If we'd known when she was a month or six months or a year... before she was walking and talking at least but I think that's nonsense. She was a person long before that. I was bound to her long before that... The thing I find most odd now is that it took such a long time for us to find out. She was three years old by the time we had the test. Three; I felt so stupid about that. Like I'd really let her down. Felt like a right idiot.

It's funny, isn't it? How having children, becoming a parent... It's one of the hardest things you ever do, I don't mean it's not great as well, of course it is, but it's tough, you know? You need to know all this stuff immediately and no one tells you anything. They don't cover it in school and all the people who have kids already are too exhausted to tell you what they know, so there's just this big gap of information and the next thing you know; there you are, looking after it twenty-four hours a day and it's not like it is low stakes or anything. Mess up and they die basically. That's what you're dealing with so, well, it's just kind of a big deal.

Isn't it insane how much time they take up? All they do is eat and sleep and wee and laugh. That's it, but somehow that takes every second of every moment of every day, including the whole of the night. How can eating and sleeping and weeing and laughing be so time-consuming?

I couldn't believe it the night she was born. They just left me with her. Like I knew what to do or something: 'Come back!' I felt like yelling. 'I don't know how to work this thing!'

I've never been very good at speaking up for myself. I'm not exactly shy but, actually that's not true, I am quite shy but it's

not because of that. It's just... I hate conflict. Avoid it at any cost.
I say yes when I'm thinking no and I keep quiet when I want to
shout. In a way it's a good thing. I think it is really because, well,
I have friends, which is, you know... and I think I'm a pretty nice
person to be around, at least I hope so.

Where we live, it's nice... it's not posh or anything but, you
know, it's not rough, it's just normal. Like we are, I suppose.
A normal house on a normal estate.

You never really realise that other people live differently to you,
do you? I mean, you know people do in theory but on a day-to-
day basis, you don't really think about it...

You think everyone is just like you are or most people are
anyway... at least that's how I think.

That's why I call my house normal because it is... how we live
is the normal way to live but other people do live differently to
us. I know that now. People live in a way that I would think
of... that most people would think of as... well, I guess
privileged is the correct word, isn't it? Privileged compared to
the rest of us plebs anyway.

That's how they lived.

I've often wondered how long it would take someone who
didn't like children to completely fall in love with one if they
had to look after it because I genuinely think they would. Like
if you got some businessman who only cared about work and
who worked in like the world's shittiest bank or something and
voted UKIP and, like he's not a nice person, that's the picture
I'm trying to paint here but I bet if he had to look after, let's say
a five-year-old for a month, night and day, day and night, on his
own... I mean, unless he was a total psycho or whatever, like
unless there was something actually wrong with him, then I bet
you anything that by the end of the month he'd be completely in
love with that child. He just would be. There is something about
the simple act of looking after them that makes you fall in love
with them. I know it's probably all biological and to do with the

continuation of the human race and stuff like that but it doesn't mean you don't feel it just as strongly.

I hadn't planned on getting pregnant when I did. That wasn't what I was planning to do at all. Had a place at uni, was going to study tourism and then maybe work abroad for a couple of years. I speak three languages, so it seemed like the obvious thing to do, and fun, you know? Not that I regret it... I wouldn't change a thing, I really wouldn't. Sometimes in life, staying still is the most exciting thing you can do. I'm sure if I had worked abroad and done all that stuff it would have been an adventure but it wouldn't have changed me; whereas having Ellie, well that turned me upside down and inside out.

There was quite a big hoo-ha when people found out. You wouldn't think it'd be all that shocking these days would you but apparently it still is. Caused a huge stir at first and then, well then, basically, everyone realised that me being pregnant meant there would be a baby in the family and after they realised that no one minded so much any more. Well, my mum did but she came round eventually. Not by the time I gave birth. Not a chance. No way, José. But by the time Ellie was six months old... she'd calmed down by then at any road.

We haven't had a child in our family for quite a while so I knew it'd be spoiled rotten from the moment it was born...

I shouldn't keep calling her 'it', should I? It's sort of my sense of humour, you know? 'Where is it? I'm sure I put it down around here somewhere,' but other people don't seem to find that sort of thing quite as funny as I do...

I can be a bit weird sometimes.

Don't you think it's funny that when you're a kid, you have all these ideas about what you're going to be when you grow up, but when you grow up you wouldn't dream of doing any of them? I was going to run an ice-cream parlour for ages... one of those diner-style ones you see in the old American movies...

had a real thing for making ice-cream sundaes for people for some reason… I am pretty amazing at it, mind… make a mean choc-nut deluxe. And then, of course, I was going to be a ski instructor. There's this brilliant indoor ski slope near where we live and I used to work there Saturdays for a while. Really got into it and thought, yes this is it, this is me but the way life changes under your feet means… well, it has always felt to me like we're not driving, if you know what I mean?

I didn't have the best labour. Young mums don't apparently. Don't know why that is. Thirty-six hours and then I didn't even manage to get her out myself after all that heaving… had to have a forceps delivery. So, when they handed her to me, all mucky and blueish with her big cone head from the forceps, I didn't feel anything… just, oh great, that's over, can I please go to sleep now? I wasn't depressed or anything. Not at all, I was fine. Freaked my midwife out a bit though I think because I wasn't all oohing and aahing and wanting to gaze into her eyes for hours on end, but I was fine, honestly; I was just really, really fucking tired.

Pete was exhausted too. He'd been up with me for two days (and been white as a sheet for most of that), so he went home to get some sleep and then he said, he was so knackered that he slept right through until eleven o'clock the next day. Hadn't meant to but that's why he wasn't there until the afternoon.

And Mum wasn't there, of course… still wasn't talking to me at that point. Perhaps if she had been, things might have been different… I do think that sometimes. Not that I blame her… I understood why she was upset with me, well I sort of did… She thought I was throwing my life away but I never saw it like that.

Having a baby, being a mum, I mean you're lucky if you get to do all that, aren't you? Not everybody does. Not by a long shot. All those people who want children, but can't, or think they'll just wait a bit longer because they've got some super-cool job and then they realise they've gone and missed the boat. I would much rather be a young mum than one of those people.

Hospitals always turn me into a proper good girl. I fall immediately into being on my best behaviour, like I'm in school or something, and I was a right goody two-shoes at school. Not because, you know, I was boring or anything. I had friends and that… I just, well, I just really liked school. Bit weird, see?

I think it happens when you first see them laugh. That's the first thing and then, well, it's all the little things, isn't it? Are they a lark or an owl? Are they jolly or grumpy? Serious or silly? You find out how tough they are, how kind they are, how bossy they are. All the important stuff.

Ellie was clever as you like, right from the start… always had this incredible knack for communicating with me. Could tell me exactly what she wanted from day one. Don't know how she did it. It wasn't like she could talk or anything but I knew she was bossing me around. Had me round her little finger she did.

She was an owl, like me, that was obvious, always perked up in the evening and never wanted to go to bed, always sluggish in the morning and she was incredibly thirsty; don't know how I knew, but I knew she wanted to breastfeed because she was thirsty not hungry. She found people falling over the most horrifying thing she'd ever seen and hated bananas and loved, I mean absolutely *loved* lawnmowers, used to jump up and down when she saw one.

People always say that children are adaptable like it's true. It's one of those things that gets trotted out as an ancient wisdom but I think it's the biggest lie in the whole world and anyone who has a child knows it. When people say they're getting divorced but it's okay because children are adaptable. Total bollocks. They know they're lying deep down. They do. They must do. Children hate change. They hate it more than anything. Even tiny changes, let alone anything big. They don't cope with it well at all. They just pretend they're okay because they want to make you happy but they're not.

The first few days back home with Ellie were a complete blur. I did what I needed to; fed her, cuddled her, tried to get her to sleep but I don't really remember anything much about it. I was too overwhelmed, I think. And then, about two days after we got back, it came: the love surge! Oh my God is that not the funniest thing in the whole world? I thought when people said after having a baby you get this love-hormone thing… I always thought that was to do with, you know, loving the baby. Ha! How wrong was I? Or maybe other people don't get it like I had it but I'm telling you I loved every living thing on God's earth; my midwife, the postman, the grumpy old lady who lives next door, Piers Morgan. Fucking everyone.

I knew it was my hormones for sure when Pete's mate Steve came over because I've always thought he was a bit of a twat but, oh my God, when I saw him in those few days after I'd given birth: I jumped up and hugged him like he was my long-lost brother. I was so unbelievably glad to see him.

Like natural ecstasy that love hormone is. So funny… I was like an actual lunatic.

Pete's always been what you might call the 'strong but silent' type. He was two years above me in school but I knew him and that because my brother was in his year. And he was gorgeous. Pete not my brother obvs. He was always a real blokey-bloke, even when he was fifteen, a proper alpha-male monkey-man. Hot, basically.

We used to hang out down the park to begin with. Just mates at first but then one day we got left, just the two of us. Fuck knows where everyone else had gone. Off home for their tea, I suppose. Or maybe they planned it? Oh my God, I never thought of that before, maybe they actually planned it.

Anyway, it was just the two of us and Pete said: 'I like your hair.' That was it. Casanova he is not but I guess he knew what he was doing because it worked, didn't it? We kissed for about two hours that night and we were boyfriend and girlfriend from then on.

Kissing is the best thing ever, isn't it? I think I like it better than chocolate. You know? Really snogging the face off someone. Best thing in the world.

Mum said it wouldn't last of course. Ever the optimist! 'He's your school boyfriend. No one ends up with their school boyfriend.' But we did last and I think we might have lasted even longer if...

'*Ah, Coulda. Woulda. Shoulda.*' That's what my mum would say. She always says it like it's some great wisdom but I happen to know she got it from an episode of *Sex and the City* so I try to take it with a pinch of salt.

One of my Turkish aunties knows this woman who adopted two children. She couldn't have any of her own but she was desperate, so they decided, after years of trying, to adopt. And my aunt says her friend absolutely adored these kids. A little brother and sister who she adopted together. Doted on them, she did. But then, as so often seems to happen in these cases, after a few years, she fell pregnant herself... had two of her own and do you know what she told my auntie? She said, she couldn't help it but she loved her biological children more. Gave them back. The adopted kids... put them in a children's home, after they'd been with her all that time. After they had been her children.

Isn't that the most awful story you've ever heard?

The day after she was born, Ellie had quite bad jaundice. Bright yellow she was, like a Minion. My midwife said it was nothing to worry about, lots of babies have jaundice when they're born and it's easy to treat, but that if she didn't have treatment right away it could develop into something more serious... It's hard not to panic when someone says something like that to you. She was so tiny and basically I'd just been told, that this beautiful little person who I'd only just met, was really ill... I had this wave of terror that I was about to lose her... started crying, couldn't help it, but the nurse told me it would be okay and calmly explained that she needed to go for this thing called phototherapy which means they go under this big red light for a few hours and that should make it better but if it didn't, then there were other things we could try.

When she told me that, all I could think about was those incubators you have in school for baby chickens when you're

learning about the circle of life… in my head that is what
I thought it would look like.

The nurse told me I could go with her to the phototherapy if
I wanted to but I felt really awful. I hadn't slept at all during the
night because I'd been so worried about looking after her on my
own and my whole body was aching. I meant to just have a
quick rest and then go see her but as soon as they took her
away, I fell instantly unconscious and it wasn't like a normal
sleep. It was more like falling into a coma and I didn't wake up
again until they brought her back to me three hours later.

It wasn't like I didn't notice anything. I know it's easy to say
that now but I do remember, at the time, thinking that her hair
looked different. It wasn't hugely obvious but I did actually say
something to the nurses. No one listened to me, of course, they
all just ignored me and said I was being silly. I should have
argued but… well, you know, it's hard to do that isn't it?

My brother's friend Craig went into town one day, just to do
a bit of shopping, pick up some bargains and that, you know,
the usual sort of thing…

He was walking out of Primark onto the main high street and
these lads started shouting at him, calling him gay basically.
Well, I mean, hello, of course he's fucking gay: he's the queen
of Hemel Hempstead. Has been since he was like, six years old.
I really thought people didn't do that sort of thing any more but
they… well, they beat him up, basically.

His head was so badly swollen that when me and Pete's mum
went to see him in hospital I didn't even recognise him.

He recovered okay and that, well his body did… and he says
he's fine now but he doesn't go shopping on his own any more.
Doesn't really do anything on his own any more. Happened in
a split second. He was just on the wrong street at the wrong time.

Pete was the first to say anything.

'She's very dark,' he said to me one day.

'What do you mean?' I said. 'Of course she's dark, I'm dark.'

'She's darker than you.'

That was all he said, grunted it, monosyllabic like.

'She's darker than you.'

I suppose she was quite dark if I'd stopped to think about it... I suppose you could see it if you looked properly but I never thought about it. Families can vary quite a lot, can't they? My friend Caz, who is Welsh; she has black hair and so has her husband and they've had two gingers; a boy and a girl, both bright orange and I am Turkish, so, you know... I just thought she'd got more of my genes than Pete's.

One night we were watching *EastEnders* and someone was cheating on someone or something and Pete just exploded... went really crazy at me...which wasn't like him to be fair. He was quite a calm person normally, not one for shouting or kicking off, I mean he could be a bit gruff sometimes, but he never lost his shit like that.

Anyway, all of a sudden, Pete stands up and starts shouting at me:

'I know she's not mine. It's bloody obvious. Anyone can see you've slept with someone else. I'm not fucking stupid, Hanna.'

I didn't know what to say... it took me a while to realise what he even meant and then when I did I was just worried Ellie would hear him. He was shouting so loudly. I kept telling him to keep the noise down. I mean, I know she wouldn't have understood but kids pick up on stuff, don't they? And then of course I got really angry with him and flew off the handle myself. Started shouting way louder than he had been. Well, you would, wouldn't you? Someone accusing you of something like that... I mean, that's proper defamation of character, isn't it? Bloody rude as well.

And then he just stood up and walked out.

'I'm going to my mum's.'

I thought he meant just for the night but he didn't. He meant he was leaving us.

Pete's mum was the one who wanted us to have a DNA test.

You don't want to hear what I said when she suggested that. Let's just say, I didn't like the idea, shall we? Felt he ought to trust me, but because I knew for sure that I was telling the truth, I just thought, well fuck it, at least it'll shut him up. I mean, I did resent having to prove it because at the end of the day he was basically saying I'd cheated on him when I hadn't... I never have. I've only ever been with Pete as it happens... not that you need to know that.

Anyway, so we go for the DNA test, me and Pete and both our mums... and that's when we found out: Pete was right, Ellie wasn't his, he'd been right all along but what we weren't expecting to find out of course was that she wasn't mine either.

PART TWO

They knew she was an alcoholic, apparently; the nurse.

Hospital Trust knew all about her history but what with the cuts and the problems they'd been having with staffing levels, they still employed her to do some of the less demanding shifts; night shifts, Sundays, that sort of thing. Stuff they couldn't get anyone else to do, basically. It was really just bad luck that we got her. Born on the wrong day of the week.

They said at the inquiry that she'd never been caught drunk or drinking at work but that's clearly absolute bollocks as far as I'm concerned. She obviously was... I mean, who would do that sort of thing if they weren't pissed?

When she was giving her statement, she kept contradicting herself about what had happened... kept making up all these stupid little excuses. They're supposed to keep the name tags on the babies' wrists at all times so this sort of thing can't happen but she said that she cut them off with a pair of scissors so the babies would get more light on their skin. I mean, as if that would make any difference. One tiny little strip of skin around their wrists. And then she said a load of nonsense about putting them in together because they looked lonely... made it sound like it was all just an innocent mistake but how many lives has she ruined? How many hearts did she break with what she did? And then she couldn't even be honest about it. Pathetic.

It's so hard for me to think about those first few hours now. Thinking about it makes my brain split in two... I remember giving birth to my daughter, I remember looking after her in the night; trying to get her to feed and holding her tiny little fingers in my hand... except, of course, that baby wasn't Ellie... I didn't do that with Ellie but I can't seem to make my brain separate the two things; so my memories are both true and false at the same time. It's called a paradox, apparently. I looked it up. My whole life is a paradox.

I slept in Ellie's bed with her the night we found out. Didn't dare leave her side for a moment, not even while I was asleep. Slept with her curled into my chest, so that when I woke during the night, I could feel she was still there, could feel her breathing next to me. Her soft, lovely skin.

My friend Carla (she's older than me, I used to babysit for her when I was a teenager), anyway, she told me when I was pregnant that I'd be amazed how loved I would feel once the baby was born and I remember not believing her because, well, because I don't feel like that about my mum, basically. We've always had a difficult relationship but Carla was right: you do feel very loved.

I remember this one night, when Ellie was about a year old… she was sleeping in our bed and I got in beside her and she went: 'Yes!' Like, she actually punched the air, cheered just to see me. That doesn't usually happen when people see me.

Pete couldn't cope. He's not good with anything emotional and… well, he just shut down basically.

When we found out at the clinic, the mums both went off on one, telling us what we should do and how we should feel about it and I could just see him, slipping back inside himself. He wouldn't even talk to me. Told his mum it was too hard.

And she wasn't being very helpful either, even though, you know, I know her really well, I mean, we lived with her for the first six months of Ellie's life, so… but when push comes to shove, she always takes his side, always has done, always will do. And though she never actually said it, I could tell she thought it was all my fault. That I should have…

And my mum was her usual bossy self, which I guess was helpful in its own way because I just did whatever she told me to; don't tell Ellie, okay; don't see Pete, okay; don't tell any of your friends what has happened, okay.

Looking back, I wonder if I'd been a bit more decisive… if I'd thought about what *I* wanted a bit more… I wonder if that would have stopped me feeling so isolated later on... but, you know, when something like this happens, it's like your map of yourself gets all messed up. I thought I knew what the world looked like, where everything was, but when I found out Ellie wasn't mine, it made me start to doubt everything. I've never been that confident anyway... I always assume other people know more than me or are just better at stuff than me but this made me so much worse...

I was in shock I guess. Kept waking up in the middle of the night poring over the details; Pete saying she was dark like that... the four of us sitting in the waiting room of the clinic that morning... the doctor telling me to sit down...

Sometimes the world is so surprising, the twist in events so... what's the word? Rubbish is the only word I can think of. It actually throws you, you know?

It was the social worker who'd been assigned to us (Sally, her name was), who first suggested we should meet the other family. Turns out they didn't live very far away, which I guess makes sense because we'd both gone to the same hospital to give birth but it still shocked the hell out of me when she said it. Like, we could have seen them somewhere already... could have bumped into them down the shops or at the cinema and not even realised it.

The other family hadn't suspected a thing, apparently. Had no idea until the hospital contacted them to come in for a DNA test. Can you imagine? I mean it was hard for us but at least, you know, at least we had a sort of build-up. At least there was a hint with us that something might be...

Don't know what I'd have done if it had happened to me the other way round. I'm pretty sure I would have freaked the fuck out.

Sally said the other family were really angry. Not with me, but with the hospital, which was pretty scary. Told me they were planning to sue.

I wouldn't even know how to sue someone. I don't even know how you find a lawyer. I mean, where do you even go to do that? The only place I've ever seen one is on TV. I literally actually don't even know how you would do that.

Sally said I didn't need to worry about any of that stuff; them suing and the inquiry... she said that was all to do with what had gone wrong in the past and meeting up was about how we were going to manage things in the future... which sort of made sense, I guess... And she did say we might get some compensation from the hospital which I didn't want to think about too much because you know, money wasn't going to make something like this any better, but the thought of it did sort of linger in the back of my head, like a crocodile lurking under the surface.

For the first meeting, Sally said it would be best if we kept it simple: so it was just me and Ellie and the little girl and her mum.

My daughter, I suppose I should say but that feels...

And Ellie's birth mother... I hate having to call her that. It just doesn't feel right. Every time I say it, even now, it makes me feel... still makes me feel... because it's basically the same as saying real mother, isn't it? And if someone else is Ellie's real mother, then what the fuck am I?

It's so frustrating that the only words available are to do with adoption... because that's not what happened to us... what happened to us is something quite different... I wish there were other words.

I'm not sure who suggested where the first meeting should be... at the time I assumed it was Sally but I'm not so sure now. Anyway, someone suggested it and, without thinking as usual, I agreed to go to their house.

It's funny isn't it, how you only ever feel jealous of things you see?

I've always loved our little house. It's the house I grew up in and it's got a sort of 1950s kitschness to it... I mean, I know that's because it's ex-council and it's a bit crap really and it's not because it's actually vintage or anything but none of that stuff ever mattered to me... it's always just felt homely and cosy and safe. Never bothered me that we didn't have a table to eat at or an upstairs bathroom or a lawn...

I guess that was one of the things that shocked me most the first time we went to theirs... just how much they had... I honestly had no idea other people had so much more than we did. When I see big houses in movies, I think that's because it's a film, not that people actually live like that, but I guess some people do... well, I know they do now, obviously.

Seven bedrooms they had. All en suite and a dining table that sat sixteen and three (three!) utility rooms... We just have the one utility room, we like to call it the 'kitchen'. And they had a boot room and a cloakroom and a games room... It was like being shown round the Cluedo board. But the thing that got me... the only thing that bothered me actually, was the garden... so much space to run around in... that made me very jealous... which I hated myself for, of course.

We followed the sat nav in the car to get there but when we started down this huge avenue with all the big houses on it, I thought we must be going the wrong way, so I actually turned around and went back... thought I'd missed a turn or something.

Then, of course, I realised that they did actually live in one of those big houses and my heart sank. It was like an extra thing I had to worry about. To feel shit about. My daughter, who was from my blood, my 'birth child'... well she'd basically won the lottery, hadn't she? Been upgraded.

And I could clearly see, as we walked up this massive gravel drive towards this huge mansion of a house, that in many ways she'd been quite lucky to be taken away from me and that was...

And not only that but this was where my Ellie had actually come from. This was where she should have been all along. Not our crappy little three-bed in Hemel.

As we stood on the doorstep, waiting for what seemed like an eternity, it was like this really loud voice in my head was yelling at me, telling me to just grab Ellie and make a run for it... get out of there while I still could… but I couldn't do it, because at the same time I was thinking that, I was also desperate to go inside… I was about to see what my child; mine and Pete's biological child; the child I had actually given birth to, was like…

It was all so confusing.

They were Asian. I was so fucking angry when she opened the door and I saw that. How the fuck could Sally let me go to the house not knowing that?

I mean… not only was I the world's worst mum for not realising for three years that I was raising someone else's kid but it turns out I was thick as pigshit as well because I was raising a child who wasn't even the same race as me and I hadn't even noticed. No wonder she was dark. I mean no fucking wonder.

When I saw that, I just wanted the ground to swallow me up, but Razina (that was the other mum's name) was standing there, looking at me, all expectant… so I just said hello and followed her inside.

Razina led us through to this huge conservatory at the back of the house. We must have gone through about fifteen rooms to get there and I remember suddenly feeling so pathetic. Like, you know when you get walked through school by a teacher, and even if it's for something good, like you're helping out with something, even if it's that, you still sort of feel like you've done something wrong and once that has happened, it's hard to get back to feeling okay again, isn't it? Like you've been made small and there's no getting big again.

We sat down at this huge wooden table, overlooking the garden, and Razina said:

'Look, Ayesha. Our guests are here.'

My birth daughter was called Ayesha.

That was…

Razina had bought like, dozens, like a crazy amount of really
posh cakes, like patisserie-type things... and she'd made proper
pots of tea and coffee and everything. Loads of different types;
green tea and jasmine tea and Darjeeling for fuck's sake.

I'm sure she meant well but God, talk about showing off: 'Look
how much money we have.'

I mean, there were far too many cakes for four people.

Ayesha was playing quietly in the corner with her back to us.
She was playing with this amazing wooden kitchen set (I mean
it was almost bigger than our actual kitchen) and I could just
tell she was one of those kids who takes a while to get used to
people.

Razina and me sat down at the table and she started asking me
all these questions; if we'd found them okay, if we'd had far to
come, all the usual sort of stuff... She seemed nice enough but
I couldn't help noticing that she was very overweight. You get
so competitive when you're in a situation like that, don't you?
There she was talking to me and being really nice and I'm just
thinking, wow, you're a lot fatter than me, so you know, at least
there is something I am better than you at...

Oh God, that's such an awful thing to admit to, isn't it? I should
edit myself but, you know, these are the things that go through
your head. They just are and I guess I was feeling sort of
protective because well, Ayesha was kind of on the plump side
too; pudgy little arms and legs she had and Ellie's always been
dead skinny, so... I should stop talking about it.

The girls started playing together almost immediately. Ellie
instigated it. She's good like that. Kids are amazing like that,
aren't they? Don't ask questions, just get stuck in:

'Hello, do you want to be friends?'

'Great. That's, that then.'

I often wish adults could be a bit more like that... wish I could
be a bit more like that...

They started cooking up some crazy food together in the little kitchen. I'm sure I heard one of them serving a worm smoothie. I'll give that one a miss, thanks, kids. All full up over here, thanks, girls.

I really wanted to go over and take a good look at Ayesha's face and her hands and her eyes, like for about six hours but I didn't dare do that in front of Razina... or in front of Ellie for that matter, not that Ellie would have understood, but I still felt that it was important for me to be... well, loyal to her, I suppose.

Ayesha looked like me but I could tell, personality wise, she was more like Pete. I could just see it. She had his tempo or something. She was reserved, still, just like Pete is. He's always been like that. Has that Kate Moss thing going on, where he never even cracks a smile, you know? He's cool, basically... not like me.

One of the oddest things for me was that Razina looked a lot like Ellie which was really weird and I think it may have been one of the reasons why I didn't question things as much as I should have done. I think it might have been...

I'm getting ahead of myself. Where was I?

Oh yes, so, we sat and talked, you know, all the usual stuff; the weather, the kids, *Strictly*...

Razina was definitely leading the conversation, I didn't know how old she was but she was a lot older than me which made it a bit like talking to one of my mum's friends.

I could tell she couldn't wait to start asking me about what had happened at the hospital... could tell she was working her way round to it, which put me very on edge. She skirted the subject a few times and then asked me what it was that had made us realise... which was really fucking awkward because... well, you know, there we were sat looking at these two little girls playing together who were, you know, not even the same colour as each other. I mean it wasn't so obvious when they were apart but side by side, you know? So, I'm sat there thinking, how the fuck did you *not* notice? That is the question, isn't it? That's more to the point, isn't it? But I didn't say that, of course.

It turns out, in fact, that both girls are mixed race. David, Razina's husband, is French and Pete's obviously English, so that does explain it a bit... I felt a bit better when I found that out.

Razina eventually got round to asking me about the hospital so I told her about the jaundice and the phototherapy... told her how tired I'd been and about my mum and Pete and about how I was on my own but... well, Razina had lost a lot of blood giving birth... haemorrhaged really badly and was in a medically induced coma for two weeks...

That was hard to hear because, well, because, it meant that she couldn't have...

That only I could have...

Once, when I was in primary school, I won this drawing competition. We had to draw a poster to help children cross the road safely. Mine was of this pheasant who became a lollipop man... It had lots of really bright colours on it because pheasants are very colourful birds and... that's not relevant!

Anyway, my poster won our class competition and then it went on to win the Year 4 competition as well and then, because the road-safety poster competition was quite a big deal at our school, the local paper came to take photos of the winners and for some reason, I was asked to go and get all the other children who had won from their classrooms and bring them to the hall for the photo... I thought I'd got everyone but it turns out, a week later, that I'd missed loads of kids and they weren't in the photo in the paper and apparently everyone was really upset with me about it and I didn't really think that was fair because I was only nine, but I still felt really ashamed... felt guilty about it for years... still do if I'm honest.

You know that feeling when something happens and you are kind of in shock and you're moving around and talking to people but you're not really with it? Like you are kind of awake but floating? That's how I felt that whole afternoon. I mean, I talked and ate cakes and watched the girls and had a tour of the house and everything but I felt like there was too much blood in my head or something because I couldn't think straight. Felt like my brain was spinning...

Now that I'm able to slow it all down and think back calmly, I sort of understand what was happening to me... I was panicking. I mean really panicking.

There I was, in this big posh house, looking at this woman, who was Ellie's actual birth mother and who looked like her and who had so much more to offer her than I had and I suddenly felt like nothing... like I had nothing to give her... that Ellie deserved better than me...

And at the same time, I was also experiencing this sudden wave of overwhelming regret for Ayesha... this little girl who I'd carried in my tummy for nine months and who I had given birth to and who looked like me and acted like Pete... I knew nothing about her and yet I already felt like we had a bond.

Even though, you know, it wasn't like it felt like she was my child or anything. The opposite in fact. I mean, her name was Ayesha and she looked and acted like a little Asian girl, she just did, the way she dressed and the way she moved and...

She had already become not the person she would have been if she'd grown up with me.

I did think about how Razina must be feeling, of course I did. I remember watching her face to see if she was as stressed out by the whole thing as I was, but she didn't seem to be... she seemed quite sure of herself in fact... had that confidence that posh people always seem to have.

I remember being relieved she wasn't angry, like Sally had said she was going to be, and thinking things could have been a lot worse. That I could have been meeting someone horrible or aggressive and she certainly wasn't that but... I didn't really understand her if I'm honest. She seemed like someone very different to me.

Over the next few weeks, we started meeting up fairly regularly. Razina and Ayesha and me and Ellie. I felt pretty weird about it to begin with. I mean, after the first meeting it wasn't like I was going to be like oh yeah, sure, let's meet all the time, that sounds fun but... do you know what? It was sort of okay... it got easier... the more we did it. I got used to having a lot of emotions when we met up. I was always completely worn out afterwards... like my heart had been doing double time or something but I did get used to it.

The girls got on really well, right from the start. They both liked to play imaginative games. They play this one game which Razina and me call the 'Rising Inflection Game'. It's so funny. One of them tells the other one what's happening in the story:

'We arrive at a river and there's a crocodile??'

And they always end the sentence on a rising inflection?? So it sounds like they're just suggesting what the story might be?? And then the other person replies with another suggestion?? It's really funny to listen to.

Most of the time we went to their house because they had so much more space than us...

They did come to ours once but it was a bit cramped and my mum was being really annoying, fussing over everyone and although Razina didn't actually say anything, I could tell she wasn't impressed. I'm probably being paranoid but I felt like she was looking at the place like it was dirty, so I didn't suggest it again.

David, Razina's husband, was never around. Razina told me that he ran this fancy members' club in London and worked really long hours and even they didn't see much of him. Pete still wasn't talking to me so there was no question of him coming.

Razina didn't talk about David very much but when she did
I could tell there was some tension there, she always said his
name like she was really pissed off with him, which to be
honest, seemed fair enough to me in a way because she was
blatantly raising Ayesha single-handedly. And, God, I knew how
hard that was so, well, I guess, it was one of the things which
we sort of bonded over, you know, because it was something
that we had in common. That we were both on our own.

The more we met: the more I felt like I was getting my head
around it all.

The girls were undoubtedly becoming friends and so were me
and Razina, in a way. I was starting to like her. She's one of
those people, who seems really abrupt when you first meet her
but is actually really nice when you get to know her better.

One afternoon, we were walking in the woods by their house,
and Razina suggested to me that it might be nice for the girls to
have a sleepover... that Ayesha could come and stay at our
house one Saturday and then maybe, the following week, Ellie
could stay at theirs.

When she said it, it seemed really natural, like an obvious next
step, I suppose, and when I got home, I checked with Sally, to
see what she thought about it and she said she thought it was
a good idea and that actually she'd already had a chat with
Razina about it, which I did think was a bit odd at the time
because I guess, in my head, I had expected us to have different
social workers or something but I suppose it made sense for one
person to deal with both families... though it was still a bit
weird that only I didn't know about that.

Anyway, I sort of pushed all those worries to the back of my
head because I knew the girls would love a sleepover and it
would mean that I would get the chance to spend a bit more
time getting to know Ayesha, give me the chance to spend some
time alone with her, because you only really get to know kids
when you look after them yourself, don't you?

Razina, very kindly (I thought at the time), suggested Ayesha could stay at ours the first weekend. She dropped her off in the afternoon on the Saturday and the plan was for her to stay the night and then we'd take her back up to her house on Sunday afternoon.

Ellie didn't really understand what a sleepover was, she'd never had one before but she was bouncing off the walls with excitement anyway and when they got to us, Ayesha was bouncing too, so they just bounced around together.

Razina was dead cool, had a quick cup of tea and then left straight away, went for the band-aid approach...

'You should be a bit more like that,' said my mum. Always so helpful.

Ayesha didn't make a fuss at all, just carried on playing with Ellie. She did come through to the kitchen after about half an hour to ask where her mum was but she seemed happy enough with the answer.

A little bit later, I took them both upstairs to show them where they would be sleeping because kids always worry about that sort of thing, don't they?

We'd made up a little bed for Ayesha in Ellie's room... It was one of those camp beds with a metal frame around the outside and it was a bit squished in beside Ellie's bed because Ellie's room isn't very big but it looked nice and cosy with all the covers on top. Ayesha wasn't sure about it though... said it was too low down and she didn't want to sleep on it but Ellie was such a good girl, she said Ayesha could have her bed and she would take the camp bed and they both seemed happy enough with that.

We had pizza for tea and cherry tomatoes (they went through two punnets, just the two of them) and then we watched *You've Been Framed* which we never normally do owing to the fact that Ellie basically thinks it's a horror movie but because Ayesha was enjoying it, she didn't mind it so much.

Ayesha was hilarious, she's got the best laugh, really chortles when she gets going she does, and it's the sort of laugh that makes other people laugh. It's infectious.

I decided to skip the bath for the night because… well it just felt a bit weird to do it, so the girls got straight into their pyjamas and that's when Ayesha started crying, said she missed her mum, said she wanted to go home. I felt so sad for her. She was only little and the whole idea of sleeping somewhere else was obviously suddenly a bit overwhelming.

Ellie was so sweet, she rubbed her back and said: 'There, there,' but then she got bored of doing that and went back downstairs to find my mum… she is only three, after all.

So then it was just me and Ayesha upstairs and she was really crying and then, I couldn't help myself, I started crying too. It was like a tidal wave. This huge surge of sadness just swept over me and I couldn't do anything to stop it…

I had let this poor little girl down so badly; I should have been there for her, every moment of her whole life but instead, I had let her down, as badly as anyone could, within twelve hours of her being born.

I felt as though everything was my fault and I was the worst mum in the world.

We were sitting like that, hugging one another when Ayesha suddenly stopped and looked up at me and said:

'Why are you crying, Hanna?'

(I'm guessing her mum doesn't usually comfort her by weeping uncontrollably into her hair) and I said:

'No reason,' and she just looked at me and said:

'You're weird, Hanna,' and I said, 'Thanks a lot,'

And then, I don't know why I did it, I wouldn't normally, but to cheer her up I started bouncing on the bed with her. We were holding hands and we weren't bouncing that high or anything but unfortunately she lost her grip, just for one second and slipped backwards off the bed. Her head must have just caught the edge of the metal frame of the camp bed. Not that hard I don't think but hard enough.

I was so worried because, you know, it's one thing to hurt your own kid, but when it's someone else's, it just feels so much worse. I scooped Ayesha up and ran downstairs with her.

Her head was bleeding so Mum got a wet tea towel and held it there for a few seconds and actually, once we'd cleaned it up we could see that the cut wasn't too bad... it stopped bleeding almost immediately and we gave her some Calpol, which I had checked she could have with Razina beforehand.

I didn't want to let Ayesha go to sleep straight away, just in case she had concussion or something, so I put Ellie to bed and kept Ayesha downstairs with me so I could keep an eye on her.

After about half an hour or so she fell asleep with her head resting on my legs and I figured I should phone Razina to let her know what had happened and well, she didn't actually say anything bad but the way she spoke to me, was... well, it was just a bit formal, I guess...

Anyway, I found out lots more about Ayesha that weekend. I discovered that she wasn't nearly as shy as she seemed when her mum was around; in fact she was quite feisty in her own way.

I found out that she laughed like a hyena and liked to walk on her tiptoes and slept with her hands above her head, just like Ellie, and that she ate sugar cubes behind your back in restaurants when you weren't looking.

She seemed much more like a person to me after that weekend... I had a much stronger sense of who she was, which rather proves my earlier point, I think, about getting to know them, but anyway...

The following weekend was a lot harder for me. I dropped Ellie off at their house on the Saturday and I tried to be like Razina and leave quickly, be cool about it but Ellie started kicking off and I ended up having to stay for over an hour before she would let me go... and then she would only agree to stay if I promised I'd come back and get her if she changed her mind.

When I got home, I didn't know what to do. I found myself clearing out the kitchen cupboards... Twenty-one years old and that's how I spend a free Saturday night. Loser or what?

I was so relieved when it got to Sunday afternoon and I was able to go get her.

She'd had a brilliant time, of course, typical, they cry their eyes out the whole time you are leaving and then laugh themselves silly the moment you've gone.

She'd loved sleeping in Ayesha's bedroom and they had eaten noodles and played in the garden and got dressed up as mermaids... she was full of it for days.

And then, because it had been okay, we ended up doing it again... a few more times, actually. Saturday-night sleepover became a regular thing... Ayesha would come and stay with us one weekend and then a few weekends later, Ellie would go and stay with them.

Long pause.

I have this theory about rich people. I think the reason not many people are rich is because, well, to get rich, you have to be kind of a cunt. That's why rich people need lawyers.

Normally, after a sleepover weekend, I would drop Ayesha back on the Sunday afternoon and get straight off (the girls were always pretty tired and I always wanted to get back myself), but for some reason, this weekend, Razina asked me to go in for a cup of tea and she was pretty insistent about it so I said fine.

We'd had a really nice time that weekend... we'd been shopping on the Saturday and I'd bought them both these little baseball caps... pink with loads of sequins on them...

It wasn't like I thought they were classy or anything, I knew they were pretty tacky, I'm not stupid, but Razina took one look at Ayesha in that cap and pulled it straight off her head, threw it down like it was embarrassing or something and that's when I knew something was up because Razina would never normally do something like that...

She led me through to the conservatory and went to put the kettle on and that's when I saw him; David. He was sat in his office with the door wide open...

It was the first time I'd ever seen him but he didn't introduce himself or anything, just sat at his desk, writing. Didn't even look up.

I looked at Razina to see if she thought it was odd of him to not say hello or anything but she was just staring at the kettle... avoiding my eyes.

And then, suddenly, it happened.

He stood up and walked towards me and I noticed he was holding this letter in his hands. I had a bad feeling about it straight away but everything happened so quickly. Too quickly for me to react.

He handed me the letter and I said: 'What's this?' and he just said, 'It's for you. You don't have to read it now. Take your time. It's from our lawyers.'

I couldn't help it... I looked straight at Razina, you know, as if to say, what the fuck? But she just stared at the floor. So I looked back at him and he looked me in the eyes and he said:

'We would like our birth daughter to live with us. It's the right thing to do. It's all in the letter.'

Have you ever had that moment? That feeling that you can suddenly see everything clearly and it is like a picture that was all blurry suddenly comes into focus and you feel like such a twat because you were looking at the thing the whole time but you didn't actually see it? Well, that's what it was like.

All the pieces suddenly fitted together and everything made sense. They'd been planning this all along: Razina, David, Sally... all of them.

And all those things I'd agreed to without actually thinking about what it meant, now seemed really stupid; the sleepovers, always going to their house like I agreed my house wasn't as good, telling Razina the truth about all the stuff that happened at the hospital...

It was like they had been planning to do this from the start... felt like they must have been. Tricking me into trusting them when all along they were planning to take my daughter away from me.

I should have said something right there and then... should have said no fucking way, that's not happening but when people ambush you like that, you just can't gather your thoughts in time... your brain just can't do it. They have the advantage, don't they, because you're the one being taken by surprise.

I can't remember anything about the drive home.

Just found myself pulling up outside our house, like no time had passed, my heart pounding and this phrase running round and round my head:

'Wolf in sheep's clothing.'

I don't even know what I meant by it. I just kept thinking it over and over:

'Wolf in sheep's clothing.'

PART THREE

I really wanted to talk to someone, to tell someone what had happened, have someone tell me what to do but when I got back Mum was out and I remembered she was working late.

I thought about going round to see Pete but we hadn't spoken for months and I didn't know how he'd react...

Thought about phoning Suze, asking her to come over, but I hadn't told her anything and I was worried she'd be pissed off with me about that.

My head was spinning with all the things that had happened; David walking towards me with the letter like that; Sally saying she thought a sleepover would be a good idea; Razina pulling the little pink cap off Ayesha's head with that look on her face.

I plonked Ellie down in front of the telly and started tidying up. Don't know why.

Was moving around in a daze, like I was on autopilot.

Couldn't think straight. Couldn't sit still. Couldn't concentrate on anything.

Found myself putting pasta on a plate without remembering making it.

Found myself sitting on the bed upstairs, staring at the letter, not knowing how I'd got there.

Didn't know what to do with it. Didn't want to open it because I knew it would upset me but, unopened, it was like this bomb that could explode at any moment.

I ripped it open in a burst, I didn't even mean to... it just happened and as soon as I started reading, I couldn't look away.

Said all this awful stuff. Kept referring to me as a 'single mother'. Brought up Ayesha cutting her head at my house like it was some huge thing. Kept going on about my 'failure to notice' the babies had been swapped like they hadn't spent three years raising the wrong child themselves. Kept talking about my 'circumstances', saying they were 'better placed' than me.

They were making out I was an unsuitable mother. Making out they could give Ellie a better home than me.

At first I couldn't work out why they were saying all that stuff... couldn't see what the point of it was... and then it dawned on me; they didn't want to swap children; they wanted them both.

I don't remember making a decision.

Just found myself packing a suitcase; grabbing loads of random stuff and chucking it into the boot of the car.

I didn't want anyone calling me, so I turned my phone off and shoved it in the glove compartment.

Got Ellie changed into her pyjamas, settled her in her car seat with her teddy and a dummy and just drove.

I had no idea where I was going.

Just wanted to get as far away as possible.

I headed straight for the M1 and aimed north. Ellie was asleep within seconds, she must have been really tired and then it was just me...

Thundering up the fast lane.

Trying to put as much distance between myself and them as possible.

There is something hypnotic about motorways, isn't there?

It's like you go into a kind of trance where you are nothing but your thoughts.

The road was like a blank sheet: a featureless nothing.

The sky was turning black and the lights of the cars coming towards me were making my eyes hurt.

A thousand questions were racing through my head.

There was so much I didn't understand.

Why hadn't I questioned why we were meeting up?

Why had I thought I could trust them?

Why the fuck hadn't Pete been around to help me with all this shit?

I was so angry with him.

Was so angry with all of them.

The way this was all happening… it was like I wasn't even going to get a say.

They were just going to take everything from me and there was nothing I could do about it.

I had never even considered…

Had never imagined…

I thought we were meeting so that we could be like, well, aunties to our birth children, I suppose… be part of their lives, of course, but I never imagined anything like this might happen.

Which just shows how stupid I am really, doesn't it?

I couldn't understand Razina. What the fuck was wrong with her?

I couldn't understand how she could do this to us.

She'd seen me and Ellie together… she knew how close we were.

If they asked Ellie what she wanted, I knew exactly what she'd say:

'I want to be with my mum.'

Because *she* knew who her mum was. She knew and I knew and I couldn't believe Razina didn't.

But little kids don't get to decide these things, do they? That's the problem. No one cares what little kids want when it comes to this sort of thing. Lawyers get to decide, fucking lawyers.

After about an hour we started getting signs for the M6 and I decided where I was going to go.

Scotland. Fort William. I'd been there once on a school trip and I remembered it was nice and I remembered it felt like it was a very, very long way away.

Just after we'd passed Birmingham, the light came on to say I needed petrol so I pulled into this service station.

I couldn't leave Ellie in the car, obviously, so I picked her up and popped her on my shoulder… managed to get her out of her car seat without waking her up. Thought I'd better go for a wee, while I had the chance, so went into the disabled loo and lay Ellie down on the baby change. She looked so sweet, fast asleep in her pyjamas on that little plastic tray, like the Cheshire cat, sleeping anywhere, oblivious to the danger she was in.

Whilst I was waiting to pay, this old man behind us said something to me about Ellie being ready for bed and I panicked so much I dropped my purse. I think he was just being friendly but the mere fact he had noticed us, terrified me. I mumbled something, can't remember what, and got out of there as quickly as I could.

Couldn't believe how fast my heart was pounding.

Decided not to stop again until we were as far away as possible.

Put the blowers on and aimed them just at me so Ellie wouldn't get cold…

Started singing to myself to try and stay awake.

The stretch from Birmingham to Glasgow was the worst. It went on forever and ever and I thought, once we got into Scotland, it would be a nicer road, but it was solid motorway all the way, four lanes wide with loads of huge lorries on it and, as if the universe was having some sort of laugh or something, the moment we crossed the border, it started pouring with rain.

I was trying really hard to concentrate but you know what it is like when you're just driving and driving like that... there's nothing to keep you alert so you just zone out.

Find yourself going faster and faster, just to stay awake.

The last part of the journey was really spacey. We were driving along the side of this huge lake, with mountains all around us and I felt like I was in a dream. The moon was really bright and it was giving everything this strange unearthly glow. I felt like I was dead already and in some other world.

We reached Fort William just before four in the morning and I suddenly realised I was exhausted.

It hit me like a train. The tension of driving like that, of feeling I had to get away.

The adrenaline or whatever it was that had kept me going so far had run out. Just like that.

I had to sleep... even if it was only for a few minutes. I had to close my eyes.

I saw this lay-by by the side of the road and pulled in.

Turned the engine off and fell asleep instantly.

Like I'd fallen unconscious.

Felt like I'd only been asleep for a second when Ellie started screaming.

Kids have a deathly instinct for knowing when you're properly tired, don't they?

There was no way she was going to go back to sleep. She was all stiff and grumpy from being in the car all night and she was hungry...

I drove round, trying to find anywhere I could get her some food but it was six in the morning and nothing was open...

Eventually I found this McDonald's that opened at seven and figured I'd just wait it out but while we were sitting in the car park, I spotted this Premier Inn just up the road.

I knew it was probably a bad idea but I was so fucking tired... I drove the hundred metres up to it and went in to ask if they had a room... The woman on the desk said they didn't normally let people check in at that time of day but I lied and said that Ellie was poorly so she let us.

The cheapest room was ninety-four pounds, just for one night. Can you believe that? I needed to sleep so badly that I didn't have any choice but fucking hell...

The room was fine. Exactly what you'd expect, nothing special, definitely not worth ninety-four pounds.

I gave Ellie some of the free biscuits to stop her going on at me and made a little sort of soft play area for her in front of the telly.

I'd brought everything up from the car including my phone and without intending to, I stupidly turned it on, out of habit, I suppose.

There were six missed calls: four from my mum and two from Razina.

I couldn't breathe.

Why the fuck was Razina calling me? Did she suspect something? She couldn't, could she?

Mum I could understand, we'd been gone all night and it's not like I'd left a note or anything.

I texted her quickly to say we were fine and that I'd taken Ellie away for a couple of days and not to worry about it...

I'd never done anything like that before but I tried to make it sound as though it was no big deal.

She must have been up, because she texted me straight back asking where we were... I wasn't sure what to say so I just said lied and said Cornwall to stop her from asking more questions... Tried to make it sound as casual as I could but, wasn't really thinking straight to be honest. She texted me back, something about: 'Promise me you won't do anything stupid' and I just thought, God she never misses a chance for a bit of drama, does she, so I didn't reply.

Razina had left a message... I didn't want to listen to it... was terrified about what she might say but I figured I'd better. Knowing it was there would only gnaw at me otherwise. 'Hi Hanna, it's Razina. I need to talk to you. Can you call me please?' What did she want? Maybe they were trying to do some good cop/bad cop thing on me.

There was no way I was going to call her back. How could I trust her? After what had happened.

I turned the phone off again and threw it into a drawer. Lay down on the bed and tried to get to sleep.

I closed my eyes but I couldn't stop thinking about everything, running it round and round in my head. Ellie was getting restless and saying she was hungry again so I gave up, took her back down to the McDonald's to get us some breakfast.

It was one of those new ones that has a play area at the end. Sat next to it and let Ellie run around so I could get a few minutes peace.

I hadn't really thought this through.

What was I doing?

I had a hundred and thirty pounds left in my bank account and no plan. No idea about what to do next.

How was I going to live? How was any of this helping?

I started hyperventilating.

I mean, really panicking.

Part of me wanted to call my mum... let her shout at me for doing something stupid and tell me to come back home but I was too scared of what would happen if I did that. Too confused about everything.

If I'd thought for a moment that there was any chance at all that I could win against them and their lawyer... that we could even get a fair shot at things, I might have gone back but there wasn't a hope in hell. I didn't stand a chance.

After breakfast, we found a Tesco Metro and I bought some food to take up to the room.

I was too bleary to actually do anything, so we spent the rest of the day inside... watched TV and ate one of those pasta things you can make up with hot water.

Managed to get Ellie off fairly early and was in bed by eight myself but I couldn't sleep... just lay there, all night with my eyes shut, never actually sleeping, not properly anyway, not falling into that deep sleep that you actually need...

It's worse than not sleeping when that happens, isn't it?

Makes you crazy dizzy.

When we finally got up the next morning, I felt more tired than ever.

My whole body felt weird, like I was getting ill or something and my head was a mess.

Got us both dressed and just sat there, staring at the wall for ages, not sure what to do.

I definitely couldn't afford another night here, that was certain, but how was I going to find somewhere else when I couldn't even think straight?

I needed a coffee to wake me up so we went back down to the McDonald's to get some breakfast.

Ellie was being really annoying. Kept asking when we were going home... kept saying she wanted to see her AnnaAnna.

I told her to shush, because obviously I didn't want anyone to hear her saying that, but she just kept going on at me.

I bought her a bottle of juice and a sausage-sandwich thing and got myself a large coffee.

Went and sat in the same place and let her run around so I could get a break from her, just for a couple of minutes...

I took out my phone to look up cheap places to stay. Thought we might be able to get a cottage or something. Thought maybe that would be cheaper than a hotel and then, I don't know, try and get a job or something I guess. Maybe sell the car even.

I had thirty-nine missed calls.

I started scrolling through my phone, frantically, to see who they were from; twelve were from my mum, eight from Razina, fifteen were from an undisclosed number, four were from Sally....

Fuck. Fuck it.

Why was everyone calling me?

Something was wrong. It had to be.

I grabbed Ellie and our stuff and stood up to leave and that's when I saw it... on the TV up in the corner of the room.

It was on BBC News, on the ticker tape thing at the bottom of the screen.

'Mother and child missing: Family concerned.'

Did that mean us?

It cut back to the newsreader who was saying something and then it came up... this picture of me and Ellie at the beach from last summer.

I pulled my hood up over my head, grabbed Ellie and got out of there as quickly as I could.

Dashed up the street to the hotel, trying to make sure no one saw us...

Ellie was in a right grump. She was crying the whole time, which was really stressing me out.

I kept yelling at her to be quiet but she was like a stuck record.

I practically threw my keys at the woman on the desk. Was in the doorway, about to leave, when she called me back. My heart nearly jumped out of my chest. I thought about running for it but figured that would only make me seem suspicious. Turns out she just wanted to tell me that the road up to Ben Nevis was closed. I mumbled thanks or something and then just pegged it.

I needed to get as far away as possible.

Needed to be somewhere else. Somewhere further away. Further north perhaps.

Someone was bound to have seen us over the last few days: that nosy old bloke in Tescos; the man at the service station on the motorway. He had spoken to us.

Loads of people probably.

I shouldn't have used my card. I should have got some money out near home and just used cash. Too late now. I'd fucked that up. And what about the car? Did I need to get rid of it? I couldn't yet. I needed to get further away first but then I was going to have to. It made me too easy to find.

I didn't know which way to go.

I saw a sign for Loch Ness. Was pretty sure that was further north so just followed it but it was a shitty, little A-road that basically followed the side of the loch, endlessly winding and twisting the whole way... making it really hard to drive... lots of hairpin bends and steep little hills.

It was raining again... that really grey, drizzly rain that Scotland specialises in. Could hardly see a thing. I was going too fast, I knew I was but I was in such a panic.

Ellie was moaning again about being hungry.

'We just ate. You can't be,' I yelled, and then she started crying because I'd shouted at her.

'Just stop crying, Ellie, will you? I need to concentrate on driving. I'm really tired.'

How did they know we were missing?

It had to be my mum. It had to be. There was no one else.

I couldn't believe even she would do that. If she'd just kept quiet, then there was no way anyone else could have found out.

'I want to go home. I want to see AnnaAnna.'

Be quiet, Ellie.

'I hate the car.'

Ellie, please, I'm trying to drive. I can't see properly. I need to concentrate.

'I want to go home.'

We can't go home.

'But I want to.'

We can't.

'But I don't like this.'

I turned around to shout at her and that's when I saw it.

This police car, coming up behind us.

I was so shocked.

They couldn't be following us, could they? How could they have found us so soon? They couldn't have.

I sped up to see if they copied me.

They did.

Shit, shit, shit, shit.

I didn't know what to do.

I couldn't outrun them but I didn't want to stop.

What if they were going to take Ellie away from me right there and then?

I was going too fast and because I kept looking behind me, I didn't see the bend until we were on it. I tried to hold onto the steering but I couldn't.

The car span right off the road, through this hedge, and started turning over and over. Rolling down the hill.

I couldn't tell where I was or which way up we were.

Felt this awful pain in my chest.

Was being really thrown around inside the car and I know I banged my head.

The car came to a halt on its side.

I was so disorientated.

Couldn't work out for a second which way up we were.

You can always tell when kids are actually hurt, can't you, because they go silent.

My head and my chest hurt really badly but I knew I had to move.

I undid my seatbelt and forced myself to climb out.

I leaned across the back seat and pulled Ellie out of her baby seat. Her body was all floppy, like she was asleep, even though her eyes were open.

I could tell she was properly hurt.

My head was throbbing.

I didn't know what to do but my instincts were telling me to keep going.

I started walking across the field with her towards the loch.

It was so quiet, like all the sound had been sucked out of the world, like I was moving in a dream.

The rain was pouring.

I felt like I was floating almost.

The field sloped down towards a cliff edge.

I walked right up to it and stood there, looking down at the icy grey water below.

Not a sound in the world, just my breath and the rain.

There was nothing I could do.

There was no way out of this.

They were going to take my daughter away from me and there was nothing I could do about it.

Nothing I could say to make them stop.

It was the end of the road.

Long pause.

I'd left the letter from David on my bed.

Poor Mum had come in from work and seen it and not known what to do.

When she sent me that text about not doing anything silly and I didn't reply to it...

Well, then she just panicked and called the police.

And then, when they worked out that I wasn't in Cornwall, like I'd said I was... that's when it had all gotten serious.

I don't blame her.

I'd have probably done the same thing.

Probably.

Ellie had broken her collar bone and I had concussion and bruising across my chest from the seat belt. I couldn't believe I'd hurt her. I felt so horribly guilty about that.

My mum flew up to Inverness to come and get us and for once I was really glad to see her.

When we got back, Social Services kept telling me that everything was okay, that they weren't going to take Ellie away from me, but I found it hard to believe them and I kept having these panic attacks.

I'm on medication for that now, which is okay, and I'm getting loads of counselling.

I think Social Services are worried I'm going to sue them or something because they're being especially helpful, which works for me.

Me and Razina had to have a formal meeting... Sally supervised it.

Razina was really honest with me about everything.

She explained that David had got that letter drawn up without talking to her first and when she found out about it. Well, she said it'd been the final straw. Said, they'd not been getting on well for ages...

He'd never even met Ellie before that day. He had no right to do what he did.

She admitted that when she'd first suggested that we have sleepovers, she *was* thinking that it might be the first step towards us swapping back... said she'd thought that to begin with, but the more time she'd spent with us, the more she realised that there was no way... that it could never happen.

She couldn't bear the thought of giving up Ayesha, so she knew I must feel the same way about Ellie.

I never knew until that conversation but Razina had gone through five rounds of IVF just to have a baby at all. They'd been on their last chance basically. Were going to give up if it didn't work out. And she'd been so grateful just to have a child. Had been so thankful that, the fact that it wasn't in the end her birth child she'd raised, well, it didn't matter so much to her.

She didn't really understand why not, she said, but that was how she felt.

There are times when I panic, when I worry if I can trust anyone because of what happened but mostly I just get on with it.

I mean at least I know now for sure that if anything did happen again, me and Ellie would be out of here like a shot...

And we'd go somewhere cleverer than Fort William next time I can tell you.

I've been watching that show, *Hunted*, and I think I would know exactly what to do if...

It won't happen, it's all good...

Razina doesn't want to take Ellie from me, she's told me that loads of times, and I don't want to take Ayesha from her.

And now, well, we're just muddling through basically.

It's not perfect but we do the best we can.

And I know it will probably sound really weird but I do think of us as a family.

Me and Ellie and Razina and Ayesha, because we are… in a way.

I mean, not a normal way obviously but…

We're linked together, we just are.

And, you know, sometimes it's good, sometimes it's hard, mostly it's just messy.

Families aren't fixed, are they? They're created and they can be anything.

They are made by people rubbing along together, looking after one another, being part of one another's lives and that bond is a hundred thousand times stronger and more important than any amount of blood or DNA or convention.

My daughter has a sister she would never have had if families were something set in stone and I wouldn't give that up for anything.

So if our set-up is a bit of an unusual one, well, who cares?

The question I get asked most often, when people find out about what happened to us, is this: if I could go back in time, would I make it not happen?

And I always shrug and give the same answer:

'*Ah – Coulda, Woulda, Shoulda.*'

A Nick Hern Book

Hanna first published in Great Britain as a paperback original in 2018
by Nick Hern Books Limited, The Glasshouse, 49a Goldhawk Road, London
W12 8QP, in association with Papatango Theatre Company

Hanna copyright © 2018 Sam Potter

Sam Potter has asserted her right to be identified as the author of this work

Cover image: Rebecca Pitt

Designed and typeset by Nick Hern Books, London
Printed in the UK by Mimeo Ltd, Huntingdon, Cambridgeshire PE29 6XX

A CIP catalogue record for this book is available from the British Library

ISBN 978 1 84842 702 0

Woodland
CARBON
www.woodlandcarbon.co.uk
NICK HERN BOOKS
Printed on Carbon Captured paper